"The Blue Eyed Side"

A Poem Novel

L.B. Sedlacek

Copyright© 2020 L.B. Sedlacek
ISBN: 978-93-88319-30-0

First Edition: 2020
Rs. 200/-

Cyberwit.net
HIG 45 Kaushambi Kunj, Kalindipuram
Allahabad - 211011 (U.P.) India
http://www.cyberwit.net
Tel: +(91) 9415091004
E-mail: info@cyberwit.net

Printed at Thomson Press India Limited.

Poem or Verse Novel:

A poem novel is a novel-length narrative

told through poetry rather than prose.

Also by LB Sedlacek

Alexandra's Wreck - Kitty Litter Press

Four Thieves of Vinegar & Other Short Stories - Alien Budda Press

Happy Little Clouds – Guerilla Genesis Press

Simultaneous Submissions - Cyberwit

The Adventures of Stick People on Cars – Alien Buddha Press

The Architect of French Fries - Presa Press

The Poet Next Door - Cyberwit

Words and Bones - Finishing Line Press

Contents

Chapter 1: A White Cat

A white cat with
only one blue eye
        usually
        experiences deafness
in one ear.

The ear is most always
        on the blue side.

Chapter 2: The Burying

In between sightings of the white
cat,
    it isn't mine
but I know whose it is
and a black dog with a white mask,
    always in the road
I swerve to keep
from hitting him with my car
I answer phone calls about my class reunion
    and where everybody's ended up
    and what last name they're using
    and what first name they aren't using
    and what last name they wish they'd
    forget (aren't we all forgotten?)

Many of the kids I used to know
never left. I left. No one knew my
name – "Mikeal," they could never
spell it. They could never say it.
Now, they know it. Everybody calls me
"Mike." Do I tell them
they're forgotten? Do I
utter "I am Mikeal not Mike?"

I work at a kite surfing shop. We rent kite
sails – surfboards with sails, at
least that's what I
call 'em. My accent is thick.
My accent's like molasses.

I've tried – I cannot shake it, I cannot lose it,
    it clings to me like
            algae, lint, syrup, kudzu
                    (the vine that ate the south) –
I read a poem about kudzu once.

We kite surf off of Hatteras on the shores
of North Carolina. There is no kudzu on Hatteras. You
have to go inland. That is what concerns me
this jibber jabber
(jabberwocky?) of mine … the inland.
It was on the inland where I had the cottage, the land
the little bit of
    swampy forest
I'd inherited from my grandparents (who raised me)
a toehold in the future
that's what they called it
    'cept they didn't think my future would begin in my
            thirties while there's got grounded fast
(I buried them in '99)
    — these things happen (that's what everybody said) while
they
    were bringing me pies and cakes and things I threw in the
river
just to see if they'd float.
Sweet potato pie floats. It
sinks
eventually.

I rented the cottage to the lady with the white cat
with the one
blue eye and the one deaf ear.
She was an actress. In town to do some

play – theater (ah, theatre!)
     She was an actress. Tall and blonde (not too many short and
fat?) and I pretended to her that I
couldn't name a show
a movie
anything she'd been in but
I've seen almost all of them, salivating.

"Mikeal" she'd say mimicking my kudzu voice, my syrupy
tongue,
     "Mikeal, could I just stay a little while longer after the play
is done? I love it so here, the people, the slowness, your syl-
lables?"

I can use the extra cash (rent is a paltry $565 a month) – it
covers
groceries, my weekly rental room at the Lighthouse Court
Motel, a game of putt putt, a bucket of oysters and
beers at the Saltee Dawgone Seafood Shack, and barbecue
(BBQ on
 the coast, it just ain't the same as in the hills, the inland –
the sauces are sweet or tart to the liking).

She pays me, she being Alexandria, going by Alexis or something
like that (I didn't keep notes on Alexis,
didn't know I'd ever need them).
I had notebooks even
and pens, lots of pens some of them
from the Lighthouse Court Motel. I keep notes in my notebooks.
I use the Lighthouse Court pens by the dozen.
I write what I remember. I write about my grandparents. About
the

murder. About who they were. With my parents
    it   was   simple
(abandonment, simple?) – it was simple.
I never knew my mother at all.
Prison and drugs. Overdoses. Suicide.
I never knew who buried her. I buried my
grandparents. In 1999. In the hills
(the mountains)
not the shores

of
North Caroline.

Chapter 3: The Bodies

My grandparents, Rachel and Ted
Jacobson. Mikeal Jacobson.
What a mouthful?
 (Mike? Oh Mike Jacobson?
Why didn't everyone
just call me Jacob?)

Rachel and Ted were from the hills. The mountains of North
Carolina. The Blue Ridge. (The mist, the legends,
the trail of tears?) Grew up there, or so they said. Did pretty
well
with the mica mines up in Plumtree (ever heard of Plumtree?,
how
'bout Spruce Pine? Burnsville? Banner Elk?) The Jacobson
Mica mine. It mined mica. The shiny silver flaky rock. You can
find
it in the mud, the woods. I found a bunch of it once outside a
forest.
It worked like a mirror, the silver creasing my reflection.
Medicines, maybe? Some kind of powder. The mine still sits
there.
 (Not on family land.) Abandoned. Toothless. Eaten up with
kudzu. (The kudzu dies and withers in the winter
turning to a rusty brown).

Rachel and Ted were miners. Plumtree was a factory town.
The homestead
was white and two stories and an eyeful for the day (some time
in the

thirties, the forties, too). It shut down, the mine, in the seventies.
With the
tax break, the money socked away (some of it saved for my
college education) –
I never did get educated.
They bought the cottage, the one I rent to Alexis, and used it for
vacations in
Columbia. A one stoplight town. A town so small you can watch
ducks crossing the highway across the waterway.
Inland. About an hour and a half from Nags Head, three from
Hatteras and
my kite surfing.

Rachel and Ted never made it to Columbia. Not permanently. A
vacation once
or twice, a scouting trip to check out the area ("Why'd you want
to live in the middle
of nowhere down near the coast?" everybody in Plumtree would
ask.)
Like Plumtree was a metropolis. There are no stoplights in
Plumtree.
Nothing to stop for. Nothing at
all. Rachel and Ted
were found in the two stories. A big bulls eye
in yellow and burgundy
painted on one side
of the house.
Rachel and Ted were found by a neighbor who walked
out to say "Hi" after he stopped at the general
store (the only one in town) for supplies.

He found the bulls eye
he found Rachel and Ted

wrapped in blankets (soaked in warm wet blood –
the bodies were still fresh, preserved in the cold,
the winters harsh in the hills of North Carolina when it's
cold enough for snow).
Somebody aimed.
The first shot paralyzed.
The second and third to
finish them off.
Each one. The
house ransacked.

My kid stuff ripped to shreds (bunny rabbit eyes
pulled from their heads).
Everybody whispered it had to do with drugs. A blip on
the news lines much like the internet sex crime
where the guy choked some woman from Maryland
while he was having sex with her and buried her in
his backyard.
All the reporters could do was talk about the hills, the hills
of North Carolina and what condition the stop signs
were in (bent, with shotgun holes, at least some of them
are). I wanted to ask them had they never been to Washington,
DC
and seen what they do to stop signs up there (if you can
find a stop sign at all).

Ted and Rachel. My grandparents. Murdered alive.
For drugs (that's what they whisper).
Some don't believe it.
Alexis doesn't believe it.
She whispers she wants to find out who did it.
She needs a good movie role. I say
but

you can't play me, you're a woman.
She says that never stops a movie maker
script writer.
Characters can be changed. Just like that.
Especially with a suitable star attached.

Chapter 4:   The Raising

I was mean. Not as a kid.
But later.
                   Much much later.
My Mom died when I was a kid.
      Maybe eleven. Twelve.
Long after it (puberty) happened.
      I couldn't cry. Voice crackled and
started …… the change.
I never knew her at all.
Ended up with my grandparents. Ted and Rachel.
Rachel and Ted. A mouse.
My Daddy (their son) – Rachel and Ted's pride and joy –
was a drunk. He'd beat me
for not fetching him a beer fast
he'd beat me for any
      reason he could think of when he could think.
Rachel and Ted bought him off.
Rachel and Ted paid him well.
      A couple of thousand (every year)
for a year or two until he drank himself underground.
      He stayed away.
Drank himself into a shadow. I got mean.
I got hard. I got exactly what I wanted. I got exactly
what I deserved.
I went east. Landed at the coast. On Hatteras
Island. Buxton. The Outer Banks.
The Lighthouse Court Motel.
I kept in touch with Ted and Rachel.
Rachel and Ted.

I got so drunk I ended up with a concussion.
I got so drunk I tripped into a commode.
I smelled like piss
I smelled like vomit
(that's what a nurse told me).

A kite surfer found me.
A kite surfer saved me.

Cleaned myself up. Cleared my mind.
Decided to revisit the story of Rachel and Ted.
Ted and Rachel.
Knowing I had to go back to Plumtree.

I fell into the toilet a week ago.
Friday night.
Just after midnight.

Chapter 5: Traveling

Plumtree (in North Carolina)
is
a block wide.
Maybe two.

A river runs
through
the middle of town
(if you can call it that) –
it's not much of a town.
The Toe River.
Don't think it has anything to do with
toes.

I don't know where it got its name.
(don't know much, do ya?)

It's wide and twisty. Maybe
good for rafting,
the white water kind.

It's off the main back road
that passes through the
mountains.

It goes to Asheville if you stay on it.

If you go the other
way to Banner Elk

they're ski resorts
and
a college.

We used to see U-Haul's
passing through all the
time.   Me and
Ted and Rachel.

I'd look at the pictures
painted on the sides.
Envious. A cowboy – Wyoming.
A cactus – Arizona.
A cow – Wisconsin.

Traveling postcards for places
I've never been.

I went to an airport once or twice
(before all the security,
before all the death)

and would pick up airline
schedules to see
where

I might go.

I never went anywhere
(even after my grandparents
offered to buy me a ticket).

I like hanging out in airports,
but I don't want to fly.

But now (because of all
the death)

you have to have a ticket
to hang out in an airport
where all the good stuff
is   (the stores, the bars, the duty free
shopping)

and that's no fun at all.

I drive a Jeep Wagoneer (the last of its kind?)

It's rugged.

It drives on through the sand.

It drives in the mud.
It drives in the ocean.

It's dark blue and some kind of wood color
(but it doesn't look like wood at all).

Chapter 6: Alexis

Alexis was a movie star.
(She starred in one
movie that was a hit —
does that count?)

Blonde. Tall. Tall and Blonde.
Those words always sound better   together.
She was tall and blonde.
Not skinny. Medium build (a few extra
pounds that weren't always there).
Green eyes. (Gotta love those green eyes!)
Short hair. Short blonde hair.
(Did I mention she was tall?)
Taller than me by a few inches.
Yes, me. Mikeal. Mike. A paltry 5' 8" to her 5' 11".
She just finished a play. (Going back to her
roots she called it. Some would call it washed up
movie star. Some would call it
disillusioned movie star. Ah theatre!)

She stands over me – Alexis – looking down.
"Where should we start?"
She looks serious. Eyebrows raised.
"In the mountains. Plumtree. It's quite a drive."
"I have time. Between gigs."
"Yeah, me too." (I'm always between gigs.)
"Who'll take care of the white cat?"
"What cat? Oh, that white one that comes around here?
It isn't mine."

I peek at the cat food in the cupboard. The cans lined up
perfectly label to label.
("We don't allow pets in the cottage" I remember telling her.)
          "Yeah, whatever. The cat that comes around here.
The white one. The one with the deaf ear. The blue eye.
I know it's not yours, but who'll feed it?"
She shrugs her shoulders. Scratches her head.
Beckons for me to sit on the sofa.
I wipe cat hair off the pillows and sit.
She had redecorated. The cottage came with a wide
olive green sofa, two matching chairs, a mirror on
the wall. This was the living room.
She added a palm tree (fake) and
a large throw rug that covered most of the polished
wood floors. A couple of pictures. Abstract. Modern.
She added a litter box
a welcome mat (inside and out).
and a small organ she bought at the weekly
flea market up in Nags Head. (Alexis can't play the organ!)
"There's the kid down the street. I'll pay him
something to do it. He likes Miss Kitty."
"How do you know she's a Miss, since she's not yours and all?"
(I remember telling her "There's no pets allowed
in the cottage.")
Alexis shrugs again.
"How do you know we'll find out anything about
who murdered your grandparents?"
          I shake my head.
Scratch my chin.
          Stare at myself in the gargantuan mirror.
My hair was black. My eyes brown. My stature skinny (next to
Alexis).
"I guess I don't know what you hope to find. It's for a

movie, right? The circumstances

to be turned into a profitable idea."

"Yeah. Sure.

It's been how long?"

"Seven years give or take a year."

"No one else wonders what happened?"

"Nope."

"Their house? It's still there?"

"Yep. No one would buy it. No one outside of Plumtree's likely

to

move there so no selling it to outsiders either."

"The story sticks?"

"Hard not to."

"Then I guess that's it?"

"That's it?"

"I'll ask the kid down the street."

"To feed the cat that's not yours?"

"Yep. And then we'll get going?"

"To Plumtree."

"To Plumtree. Where it started."

"Yep."

"What about your job?"

"The kite surfing?"

"Uh-huh?"

She pulls out a cigarette. Holds the pack out to me.

I take one and plop it in my mouth chewing hard on one end.

"I'll take a leave of absence. It's winter anyway.

   Most people aren't used to the cold water.

The cold Atlantic. Cold Pamlico sound.

Things are slow now anyway."

"I just gotta pack a few things."

"Yeah, me too."

I stare at Alexis. She was at least twelve years older than me.
I wonder if she knew that.
"Pick you up tomorrow?"
"Great."
I pet the white cat on the way out. I wipe my feet on the
welcome mat. Climb into the Wagoneer.
I wave, but no one waves to me.

Chapter 7: The Theory

I know a lot of pharmacists. Knew.
Know. Everyone does? But
personally? Personally! How personal
it can get when you're popping pills in the mouth
for all kinds of things (high blood pressure,
cholesterol, diabetes, allergies, acid reflux, arthritis, colitis,
Crohn's disease) there's always a medicine
or vitamin, or min—, nah maybe an herb? I
knew a pharmacist. Glasses. Greasy hair. He committed
suicide when his pharmacy closed. He didn't own it. Couldn't
find
a job elsewhere? Where do you look after so
many years? The mining jobs dried up in Plumtree. Everyone
started commuting to Spruce Pine, Burnsville ... eventually to
Asheville. He jumped from a cliff. Above where the
public pool used to be. In the seventies when Plumtree was all
that! All that? Who says "all that" anymore? I'm stuck in
the past! Kite surfing. Who does this for a living?
He jumped from a cliff. He was sick anyway, that's what
everyone said. No family. Living in Plumtree for the
work. The job. The mountain stream views?
You'll never taste water as fresh and clear
as from the Toe River – as weird as that
sounds.

I knew another pharmacist. The guy who took the
suicide pharmacist's job. Guess
what happened to him? (He committed suicide!) Too?
Too!

He committed suicide. One more violent. One more
quick. One that didn't leave his limbs
quivering in front of ducks and children walking
by the man made pond filled in where the public
pool used to be.
He was in trouble. Married, too.
Sneaking prescriptions to his wife.
(She had a boyfriend on the side,
someone whispered once).
He stopped giving her drugs.
Then he just stopped moving one day.
It happened a couple of months before Rachel
and Ted.
The drugstore bordered their homestead land
their driveway ran right by it
they owned the land
they owned the store.
The Plumtree Pharmaceutical.
It closed after the second pharmacist suicide.
(Two pharmacists commit suicide in
a row?)
(Two pharmacists commit suicide in
a two block town called Plumtree?)
A drug theory was born. Ted and Rachel's
murder caused by drugs.   The Sheriff said the
perpetrators thought Ted and Rachel had the inventory.
The drugs stored in their cellar.
What a place for a prescription –
damp, cold, dark, deserted.

Chapter 8: The Drive

"I can drive you know."
Alexis smiles and grins and
swings her blonde hair back and forth.
It's too short.
It doesn't swish much.
I can't help wondering
what else she might swish.

"She's too old for you"
I whisper in my head.

"Dunno. I've never let anyone drive the Wagoneer."
"You say that like's its priceless. An antique."
"They don't make 'em anymore."
"No?" She bobs her head.
I watch a few strands
of blonde hair swish into her eyes.
She wipes them away with a flick of her hand.
"All cars look the same to me."
"Yeah. Well. They're not all the same."

I flip on the radio. Alexis rolls her eyes and
stops on an oldies station.
Alexis raises her eyebrows.

"Yeah, I can get into this kind of music."
"This kind of music? Are you implying that I'm old?"

She laughs. That throaty laugh. That laugh like she's smoked
one too many cigarette
drank too much bourbon
or whiskey on New Year's Eve.

"Nah. No way. What are you? Ten years older?
If even that."

"Close enough. That's close enough."
She turns to the window. She stares out the window.

Highway 64. 64. Highway 64.
"Not much to see is there?"
"Not unless you like green. Green grass. Green trees.
Cornfields. Produce stands. Tobacco leaves."
"Yep, there's lots of that here, I guess."
"Yep. You'd think cigarettes would be cheaper in
North Carolina as they grow the stuff here."
"Maybe they are."
"Marginally. You'd have to go to a
discount warehouse.
Sales warehouse. There's nothing like that on Nag's Head.
Certainly not in Columbia."

"Columbia's a one stoplight town. Pigs. That's what this area's
big for. 'Course that one hurricane nearly wiped that out. I
heard
they had pig carcasses floating in the water for days. The smell.
The dysentery. The health hazards."

"How long's this gonna take?"
She sighs.

She's too old for you.
She's too old for you.
She's just too old.

"Dunno. A few hours. Plumtree's in the mountains. On the
other side
of the state. Eight or nine hours probably. Depends on when we
stop.
We'll have to stop for gas. Something to eat maybe.
Did you bring something to read?"
She shakes her head.
The blonde hair whisks around her face
her lips.
"I can't read in the car.
I only have scripts with me.
I could get a book or a paper."
"Yeah, convenience stores sell some of both. Don't know what
kind
of paperbacks they'll offer."
"Romance novels. You can always find those. I was on location
once.
in Africa. In the middle of nowhere. You probably haven't seen
the film."
"You mean the one where you played a farmer's wife?"

She raises her eyebrows
flicks her hair.

"You've seen it? I didn't think anyone saw it. It went straight to
video."
"You can't rent videos anymore."
"That sucks. What if you want to watch something that's only
on video?

I still have a VCR. I use it. Not much. I like having the option."
"Options. Those are good. I don't have a VCR anymore. I think I watched
it. That movie. Your movie. What was it called? We watched it at a buddies place."

She's too old for you.
She's too old for you.
She's just too old.

"Your buddies, they liked it cause I took my shirt off?"
"You took your—."

She raises her eyebrows
squints her eyes.
"Like you haven't seen it."
"Okay, I've seen it. I liked it."

She's too old for you.
She's way too old for you.
She's out of
your league so don't even
step up to the plate.
Don't even try it.

I press the brakes. Stop and wait for the light to change.
We are only in Rocky Mount.
Almost six more hours to go.

"I saw the movie. I watched you take your shirt off.
I liked it.
Okay I liked it." I smack my lips and sigh.
"You were saying about romance novels?"

She shrugs her shoulder
smoothes back her hair with her hands.

"I was on location. In the middle of nowhere. Africa.
That movie where I played a farmer's wife."
"You were on location. Got it."
"I found books. In English. Paperbacks. Romance novels. Of
every kind.
Cheap too. Something like three or four for a dollar."
"Did you stock up?"
"No. I bought one. Never finished it."

"What did you do on your free time?"
"Slept. Tried the local cuisine.
Sightseeing. What else was there to do?"

She's too old for you.
She's too old for you.
She's just too old.

I nod my head and laugh.
"Yeah. That's what I do now on Hatteras
except for the kite surfing."

She whispers,
"What else is there to do?"

Chapter 9: Hot Spots

They can happen anytime of the year.

"I don't think I've ever eaten in a place quite like this."
Alexis pulls out a cigarette. I raise my eyebrows.
She ignores me. Puffs in my face.
"What? C'mon. This place smells like a chimney."
We sit at a booth with yellow seats
more like puke orange seats
we sit at a booth the
same color as the waitress's uniform.
I order pancakes
I order bacon.
Alexis orders coffee
Alexis orders a pork chop sandwich with pickles
hold the mayo
hold the grease (can they do that?
she asks wrinkling her nose).
No one answers.

A hot spot is a localized area of
skin inflammation and/or infection.

"You like pancakes, huh?"
"Uh-huh." I pour syrup on my pancakes. I drown them.
"You're getting syrup on your bacon."
"That's okay."
She wrinkles her mouth. "You'd probably like some of
that sweet
cut bacon. I can't remember where I had it,

but I know I have.”
“Yep. Probably.”
I nod at a couple of truck drivers across the room.
“You know those guys?”
I smirk. “No. It’s just a guy thing. You know the guy nod.
Besides,
they’re more interested in you. I’m just given them
the acknowledgement
so they don’t think I’m sitting over here
thinking I’m all better than them
because I’m with a—.”
I suck on some pancake.
She doesn’t let me get away with it.
She pours cream in her coffee
she stirs and stares at me with each flick of
her spoon, each caress of the white into the brown.
“With a what?”
“Ah, c’mon you know.”
“What? You’re with a what? Mike. Mikey.
What’s your real name? Mikeal?”
I suck on bacon. “Yeah. Fine. You’re pretty.
That’s why they look. You know
that. You should. You’re an actress.”
“Were. Is that what you were thinking?”
She sips her coffee. Purses her lips.
“You’re doing the play. You’re an actress.
Some of your movies have a cult following.”
“The bad ones?”
“The ones where I take my shirt off?”
I shrug my shoulders. Suck on my water.

Hot spots are common skin lesions
that are usually caused (and made
worse) by biting, licking, or scratching.

"A guy thing. I guess I get it."
I nod. I look at the table.
I try to disappear in the crevices
I try to disappear into the cracks.
"You really think this could be a screenplay?
Someone would want to see this."
She laughs. That deep throaty laugh.
"Sure. Not you. I don't think you'd want to
see something
so
personal
onscreen, but other people would watch it.
"Why is something like this so interesting?"
"Intrigue. Unsolved murder. Real life. You
want to know what happened, too don't you?
You don't believe the
story. The drug angle.
Someone wanted an illegal prescription
wanted the key to the pharmacy. Why not break into the
pharmacy? It was near the house. Just get a rock
from the river
conveniently
running right beside the store, or scrounge up
a brick or block of cement from the mine across the street
wrap it in a blanket,
jacket, towel and break in the window.
There were numerous windows.
Glass in the door. Why go to all the trouble of the murders?
It makes no sense.
Who really had to gain?

I lift my eyes from the table.
"How did you—? You've done your

research. I thought you didn't know anything—."
"I didn't want to tell you what I knew in case you knew some-
thing
I didn't."
"But you sound like you're studying to be a private detective.
Did you hire one?"
I did the research myself. I was curious. Bored maybe
sitting about what would've been their (Ted and Rachel's)
summer
house. You told me about it when I first rented the house from
you
in Columbia or were you too
drunk to remember?"

I look at my arms.
They are tan.
They are dark next to hers, next
to Alexis's bare white skin and light brown freckles.

The important thing
for successful long term treatment
of a hot spot is to
find the underlying cause to
break the cycle.

The underlying cause
to
break
the
cycle.

The important thing is to
break the cycle.

Chapter 10: The Shade and the Shift

Back in the Wagoneer. Alexis pops the hatch.
Pulls a hairbrush from her bag. I watch her brush
her short blonde hair. She winks at me. Pulls out
a folder. "See, I've done some homework."
"Ah ha!"
"You get it?" She laughs. That deep throaty laugh.
"You didn't just find the summer home?
It was no accident."
"A real estate agent in Manteo did point you my way."
"I did wonder why you wanted to commute
to the theatre. An hour's drive. Sometimes longer if
you take the draw bridge. I figured you being who you are
you wanted your privacy.
Manteo's small.
Manteo's an island. Small community."
"I read the story. About the murders.
Something always stuck in my mind.
You seem like a nice guy Mike. Mikeal.
What is it this week?"
"Mike's fine."
"For a surfer dude."
"Kite surfer dude."
"Living in a motel."

She slams the hatch
hands me the folder
I open it and shut it just as fast.

"Don't wanna see those photos again, do ya?"
"No."

I scratch my head. Pull a baseball cap out from
under my seat. Put it on. Adjust it
in the rearview mirror. "Once was enough.
I had to be there. At the autopsy. It
was terrible."
"Yeah. I know. I'm going over the facts. The leads.
What I could scrounge up."
"Scrounge up?"
"They had work done on their house."
"Lots of people do."
"But from someone outside of the area. Not a local."
"Not unheard of."
"But no one knows who it was."
She opens the folder
flips the pages.
"The work that was done. Painting maybe. A new door. Noth-
ing
unusual. Maybe giving a drifter some work, some cash.
Maybe giving a drifter a hot meal, their lives.
It was in the file."
"Someone works on the house and wants something more.
Someone works on the house and sees something?"
"Yeah, but." She smiles. Nudges me with her elbow. "Red
light."
I slam on the brakes. "Look at it from a different angle. In
acting,
depends on if your technique or method but with
technique – that's what I use – you
make up a history of the character. The characters'
thoughts, words, how they talk, relatives,
dislikes, likes, hopes, dreams. Shaping an imaginary
person."
"You're a pretty good actor. Or should I say actress?"

"Either one will do. It's like
this.
What if—."
"Yeah?"
"What if Rachel or Ted—."
"Ted or Rachel."
"Saw something. What if they saw something they shouldn't?
And
it has to do with the mysterious worker or workers on the
house?"
"What if they didn't?
What if
it
was
nothing at all?"
"They were murdered."
"Yeah."
"What if it was a drifter?"
"What if it wasn't?"
"What if?"

Chapter 11: Girls in Trucks

Sixteen country songs in
I stop counting and
sixteen country songs in I mumble
"I think we're a couple of hours outside
of Charlotte."
Alexis sighs
Alexis paws through the glove box.
I wink at her
she acts like she doesn't notice.
"You don't even have a map of North Carolina in here. We should
stop at a welcome center."
"Could be hard to do."
"Oh yeah?"
"There's one in Columbia."
"Yeah, I know."
"And one if you come up the opposite way from New Bern."
"Yeah, I know."

"Isn't there one in the mountains? Where we're going?"
"Don't know. Don't think so. There won't be one in Plumtree.
There's
probably a welcome center or visitors center in Boone. There used to
be. There are places like that near the ski resorts. We have to pass
near one on the way. I guess we'll pass more than one."
"Does the weather get bad?"
"Bad?"

"Too bad to drive? Most people have trucks or SUVs?"
"Don't know. It depends on how many seasons they see. If they
come up just for the summer like some Floridians do
then they could drive just about anything.
Maybe even a scooter or a skateboard."
Alexis shakes her head.
"Why do people always think that everybody
in California, Hollywood especially, is always on a skateboard
or scooter or in line skates? Huh? Why is that?"
I laugh. "Don't know. It's the same as thinking every surfer
says dude."

Alexis scratches her chin.

"Don't think I've ever heard you use dude."

I nod, I stare out the windshield.
Alexis nods
Alexis stares out the windshield.
We both stare for awhile.

I like staring out the windshield.

Alexis smacks her lips
Alexis plays with the folder.
"Do you want to hear more?"
"More?"

I wink at her. She doesn't see me.
Did she just pretend she didn't see me?
"About Ted and Rachel."
"Right. More. There's always more."

"You don't take it seriously?"
I roll my eyes.
"I'm driving there, taking my surfer dude self away from the
waves. C'mon."
"Okay. Fine. Do you remember the bit about the truck?"
I shake my head.
"This truck. It was blue. Light blue. They found it abandoned
across
the river – the Toe River – from Rachel and Ted's house. It
wasn't far.
But with no way across the river … anyway. It was parked in
front of
an old general store. But this one was
abandoned across from a church
this light blue truck was
just on the other side of the street. Do you remember?"
I still shake my head. Wonder about my wink. Did she really not
see me?
"They found a body. Inside the tool chest. In the
back. Folded up. A woman. Roughly five foot two. With black
hair.
Fair. The truck had been there a week before someone reported
it to
the sheriff's office. She'd been reported missing from
another state. The tags changed to North Carolina. They
questioned Rachel and Ted. The only people living close by.
The other nearby structures — the store, the mine, the aban-
doned
store, the post office and the church. No one saw a thing.
Neither
did Rachel and Ted. That happened …. She opens the folder.
Flips and flips the pages. It happened three months
before Rachel and Ted.

Ted and Rachel.
I scratch my chin.
I wink at Alexis.
She turns her head. I don't think she noticed.
 "You think this has to do with the work on the house?"
"A truck with a tool box. Maybe."
"Who was the woman?"
"Let's see." She licks her fingers. Flips the pages.
Flips and flips the pages.
I wink at her.
She stares at me.
Turns her head.
Pretends she doesn't notice.
"She was identified. I don't have the name.
They never caught the culprit. An unsolved case.
You'd think someone would've figured it out by now."
I turn the radio back to the oldies.
"Guess it doesn't matter to the authorities.
I'd never even heard of it. Plumtree's small. But I haven't
been up there in a while. Rachel and Ted didn't call.
I never write letters or anything. They weren't into
email. Didn't own a computer."
"She was from out of state. Tennessee. I guess that's
where the case went. No one here worried about it."
"You think the two are related?"
"Possibly. Work done on the house the same time
the truck and body show up. It has to do with something."
"It always does."

I wink at her.
She turns her head
but before she does
she winks back at me.

Chapter 12: Boys in Trucks

"You want to drive?" I look at Alexis. She smirks.
"I'm not answering that."
"Why? Why not?"
The traffic picks up and
we are somewhere on the other side of Charlotte
somewhere past nowhere.
"You love this thing. This old heap of junk. What'd you call it?"
"A Wagoneer."
"Don't make those anymore, do they? These old junk
cars especially station wagons are real popular in L.A."
"Beats driving a limo? Why would that be?
You'd think they'd want
the latest, greatest, most gadget filled cars available."
"You'd think."
"What kind of car do you drive?"
"You've seen it."
"That pick up truck you have parked
at the cabin in Columbia? Come on. You're an
actress. A movie star. You made some
big bucks, didn't you?"
"I guess so. But I never see it. Never saw it.
The money gets divided up.
Managers. Publicists.
Dresses. Houses.
Bad relationships.
You name it. It's gone."
"That old blue pick up is all you have left?"
She shakes her head
flings strands of her hair out of her eyes.

"I have a house in L.A. Investments.
The truck wasn't mine to begin with."
"Why are we talking about trucks?"
"The woman in the truck
who was murdered in Plumtree?"
"The truck belonged to
you were about to tell me.
Your truck parked back in Columbia."
She pointed to a semi trailing us on the interstate.
"A guy. He stole my jewelry. I took him to court.
I said he could keep it or not return it or
not give me the cash if I could keep the truck."
"He gave up his truck. To you?"
"Yep. Signed over the title and everything."
"Do many women drive trucks?"
"There's more than you think."
"I don't know if they ever determined
that the woman killed in Plumtree —
it was in the town square, if you can call it that – ever,
no not ever, it wasn't determined who owned the truck. It
wasn't hers.
It wasn't hers, that I remember. Maybe they did find out.
Maybe it belonged to a relative or something. The truck."
"Or something. It's always something."
"Yep."
She closes her eyes
I stare straight ahead and
I think of the semi, and Alexis'
truck and the truck and the murdered woman
and the work done on the
house that belonged to Rachel and Ted, Ted and Rachel.
"Where are we anyway?"
"A few more hours. We'll be there."

"Are we gonna stay there?"
She sits up. Her eyes open wide.
"In the old house?"
"Nah. It's boarded up anyway. I'm killing two
stones here anyway."
"Two stones?"
"Two birds. Two stones. Two murders. Two trucks.
Someone wants to buy the property. Maybe. After all
these years. Make it into a spa or something."
"All the way in Plumtree in the middle of nowhere?"
"Yep. Closer to stuff than you think. Small towns, yeah, but
plenty of
summer residents, skiers and tourists.
They'd probably love a spa."
"You didn't answer my question."
I sigh
I look in the rearview mirror
reach down to adjust myself
stopping my hand telling myself I need to wait until the rest stop.
"I made a reservation at an Inn on Beech Mountain.
It's about an hour from Plumtree."
She smacks her lips.
"How many rooms?"
I laugh. Fiddle with the rearview mirror.
"Two, of course."
Two stones
two birds
two murders
two trucks
two rooms.
"How many do you need?"
She grins and
shakes her head.

"The Inn has a pool, a fireplace in every room
breakfast is included."
"Not as nice as the Lighthouse Court Motel?"
"A portajohn would be nicer."
She purses her lips. I watch her stretch.
"Wake me up if I fall asleep."
I stare out the window. The sun turns into night.
The semis blaze by on the opposite side. I watch
the headlights. I look for station wagons.
I look for women or men in pick ups and
count how many I see of each one.
"They don't make these Wagoneers anymore?"
"Nah. Newer version of.
Bigger. Larger. Faster."
"It's a classic?"
"Guess so."
"A keeper."
"Definitely."
"But it's not a truck."
"You should know."

Chapter 13: Fish or Chicken?

I carry our bags when we arrive at the Inn.
It is half full. The parking lot half empty.
The air crisp.
A mountain view all around. Green. Blue
Sky. Trees.
Alexis whistles. Smiles. Sighs.
"Clean air. No smog. No fog. No smog
burned into the fog. Just pure clean mountain air."
"You should taste the water."
She laughs. A deep throaty laugh.
"With dinner, maybe? Is that included?"
"Nope. But we can order it. There's a restaurant.
A dining room. I've made reservations."
"Guess you've thought of everything."
She winks at me.
Alexis
whistles.
Smiles.
Sighs.
"Nah. Not everything."
"Here we are."
Alexis has room 6. I have room 7.
"Nicer than the Lighthouse Court Motel?"
"It couldn't be more nice. I bet the sheets
are clean. The towels freshly laundered.
The floor vacuumed."
"But no sand between the covers."
"Nope."
I set her bag down on the floor.

Both rooms were identical: one queen size
bed, a desk, two chairs, a dresser with a large
TV, a small refrigerator, a coffee maker, and
a nightstand with an alarm clock.
"No phones." "Do you need to make a call?"
Alexis shakes her head. "Nothing to call about.
No secrets here. Nothing my agent needs to know
about." "You have one of those? I guess you'd have to."
"Yep. Even for a play. It helps with the negotiations."
I open the bathroom door. Pull out the shower curtain.
"All clear!"
Alexis slaps her hands on her ears. "Mike. C'mon. That's
not funny. What're you up to?"
"Nothing. Come on. You didn't think I had some motive.
Up to? Not a thing. I couldn't sneak around you anyway.
You're too smart."
She flops on the bed. Sits back on a pillow.
Alexis whistles.
Smiles. Sighs.
"What's for dinner? What'd they serve here?"
I shrug my shoulders. "Fish. Chicken. Some kind of turkey.
I'd have to get the menu. See if I can translate it or not. I'm not
into gourmet."
"That's all they have?"
"Yep. But I may not be reading the menu correctly. There may
be
more to it than I can tell." "A food code?"
I shrug my head to one side. "Maybe. There's been codes
found in
many lesser things."
Alexis nods. "And none of it made any sense, right?"
I shake my head. "Except for the chicken dish, no."
Alexis whistles. Smiles. Sighs.

Chapter 14: Like It's 1999

The day the solar wind almost disappeared – May 11, 1999.
Tornado in Oklahoma – May 3, 1999.
Earthquake in Kocaeli, Turkey - August 17, 1999.

1999 (MCMXCIX).
A common year.
Started on a friday.
The year of the cancer, the crab.

345 prisoners escape from Putim prison through the front gate,
Brazil – June 6, 1999.
A tornado rips through downtown Salt Lake City, Utah – August
11, 1999.
Chi-Chi earthquake kills about 2,400 people, Taiwan – September
21, 1999.

Kalispell Center Mall Armwrestling Classic, Kalispell, MT -
January 9, 1999.
14th World Hot Air Balloon Championship, Austria – August 28th
– Sept 5th, 1999.
Rachel and Ted murdered – March 11, 1999.

The 6 billionth person in the world is born in Sarajevo, Bosnia and
Herzegovina – October 12, 1999.

Chapter 15: Alexis, Part 2

Alexandria "Alexis" Russell
SAG / AFTRA
Height: 5'11"
Weight: 135 lbs.
Eyes: Blue
Hair: Blonde

<u>Film (Partial List)</u>
Flight to Nowhere   Carbonation Productions Co.
Free to Move   Star Quality Films
High and Away in the Clouds   Lead Actress Productions, LLC
Brains to Ski and Swim   Living High Films
Magic in the Air and On   Magic Air Co., LLC

<u>Television</u>
Hoops and Ice Skaters   Guest Star   Up There Television
Kayaks and Kites and Such (Pilot)   Principle   Such
Productions, LLC.

<u>Theater</u>
The Merchant of Venice
Much Ado About Nothing
Twelfth Night
A Midsummer's Night Dream
The Seagull
The Wild Duck

<u>Commercials</u>   List available upon request

<u>Training</u>
J.P. Long   Method Acting Studies   Los Angeles,
California

<u>Specials Skills</u>
Swimming, Knitting, Horse Back Riding, Golf, Knife Throwing,
Volleyball

Chapter 16: Donuts and Bagels

It is early. Early for me. An hour before
I am usually up.
Alexis is cheerful
Alexis is a morning person
Alexis carries her folder
Alexis carriers her folder, a bagel and the keys to my Wagoneer.
"What about breakfast?"
She smirks.
"Have you been asleep all this time? Don't the kite
surfers start earlier than this?"
"I'm not kite surfing. I just work there. I kite surf sometimes.
This doesn't have to do with kite surfing."
Alexis wears a black sweatshirt
Alexis wears jeans
Alexis wears black boots.
"You've been to breakfast?" "Yep. It ended hours ago.
They're
not waiting for you to get up. I saved you a donut and a bagel."
She produces two large napkins. "And some cereal and milk. I
don't know what you like for breakfast." "Doesn't matter."
I take a bite of the bagel.
It is cold
it is chewy.
I sniff the donut. It has chocolate frosting.
"What did you have?"
She plops on my unmade bed
she looks around the room.
"The same. Plus an orange. Vitamin C."
I nod and take another bite of the bagel. "How'd you sleep?"

She stares at me and sighs. "It's windy here.
Kept me up. I watched some movie – no, it wasn't one
of mine – until I fell asleep. How about you?"
"The wind doesn't bother me. It's windy on Hatteras
much of the time."
"Yep. I'm staying too far inland."
She rips open her folder
she pages through the contents.
"How far is Plumtree?"
I look at my watch
I run my fingers through my hair. "Don't know.
An hour or less. It won't take long. It's not that far from here.
You're ready to get started?"
She looks at me. "You're still in your clothes from yesterday."
I shake my head. "You don't want to wait for me to take a
shower?"
She bites her lip and sighs. "No. Be quick. I'll wait.
I can go over my file. I need to find something for notes.
Did you bring a camera?"
I shake my head. "Don't own one. Don't you? Didn't you?"
She shrugs her shoulders. "Yeah, I ought to have one."
She glances at her folder.
I finish the bagel
I fill a plastic cup with tap water.
"Did they have any juice? Coffee?"
She scrunches her lips. "Coffee. I think the coffee pot's on
all day long. I can get you a cup while you get ready. Or
try to use the coffee maker in the room if I have to.
How do you like it?" "Black. No decaf. I need to stay awake."
"Sure thing."
She stacks up the papers and stuffs them back in the folder.
Alexis is cheerful
Alexis is a morning person.

(I really hate morning people.)
Alexis shuts her folder.
"Mike?"
"Yep?"
"Thanks for letting me come along."
I pull a sweater and jeans from my bag.
"It's nice to have the company."
She stands
she walks to the door. "Alexis?"
"Yeah?" "I haven't been back."
She raises her eyebrows.
"You haven't been back?"
I nod. "Not since it happened."
She moves across the carpet
She holds out her hand.
"It'll be okay."
"Yeah?"
"Yeah."

Chapter 17: The Road to Plumtree

The road is windy. Too windy for the jeep. I take the curves in
small amounts. The brakes squeak when I tap them. Alexis
reads her folder. Alexis glances at the speedometer. Alexis
sighs. "You want to drive? You know how windy it is."
"No. I mean yes I know how windy it is." I watch the
speedometer. I am going 30 mph. A little over the speed
limit in some places. A little under in others. We travel
on 19E. The road is windy. Alexis sighs. Alexis looks at her
watch. "How much further?" "Not that far." "You know
it's hard to even find Plumtree on the map. If you didn't
know where the town of Spruce Pine was, I doubt anyone
would ever go through it." "Yep. Like I said there's a post
office. Not much else. A church or two. Some spruce pine
farms. Tree farms. An RV park used to be a bit down the
road. The Toe River runs by the road. It's pretty country.
Mostly farms. Not much else." Alexis digs through the folder.
"How long were your grandparents married?" I scratch my
chin. "Not sure. They married young, I think. She
was only sixteen." "Did they have any other children besides
your—? Was your mother or your father their child?" "My
father. Nope. No other brothers and sisters. No aunts and
uncles for me. If that'd been the case, I'd probably would
have wound up with one of them."
She nods. "Yeah. Right. Makes sense. Where were you
living when your mother—?" "In North Carolina. Outside of
Raleigh. Dad worked for the government so that's where we
ended up." "You weren't there very long, though, before you
were back here?" "No." I tap my fingers on
the steering wheel. I watch a couple of kids on four wheelers

spinning out of control in a dormant corn field.
The road is windy.
Too windy for the jeep.
"Did your grandparents have any
brothers or sisters?" "At least one brother. I never
met him. He moved up north or something. He had a falling
out with my grandfather. I'm not sure if Ted would've
recognized him if he'd come to visit. Rachel wouldn't have.
She never met Ted's brother." "How are you related to Ted's
brother?" "He would've been my great Uncle. I've been
told he passed away some time ago." She shrugs her shoulders.
"You have no idea if he had children? And if he did if his
children had children or what?" I shake my head. Nope.
The road is windy. Too windy for the jeep.
I slow down as we pass through a
school crossing. "It's Saturday. There's no school today."
"Yeah, well. Can't be too careful." "You were right.
This area makes Columbia look like a bustling town."
"Columbia's on the way to Nags Head if you're driving
from the east. That's what keeps it going. The
pig farming hasn't rebounded to what it was
after the last bad hurricane."
"Maybe all this has to do with the mysterious brother."
"I wouldn't call him mysterious." I sniff the air. We
smell like hotel pastries. "Did you see a paper today?" "There
was one in the lobby, but I just glanced at it. Why?" "Just
wondering about the weather." Alexis giggles. "I don't think you
have to worry about that as slow as you're driving." I grimace.
The road is windy. Too windy for the jeep.

Chapter 18: Plumtree

It looks the same. The post office. The tree farms.
The churches. The old general store. Abandoned.
The town square. Now a parking lot for the church.
The drug store. Now a feed store. The mine. Still
closed and abandoned. Gaping holes
in the cinder blocks. Kudzu swarming all over.
The graveyard high up on the hill overlooking the
town. The Toe River creeping lazily along as if
nothing ever happened at all.
"Ted and Rachel Jacobson. I see you chose the
double plot."
"There was a special. Buy one headstone get
one free."
Alexis giggles. Slams her fist in her mouth.
Shuffles her feet among the leaves. "Mikeal.
Mike. That's not funny. I mean. Okay, it is, but."
I laugh. "It is funny. I just thought they'd like it
better. I was talked into it. Who wants
to put a lot of thought into that when it happens?
It's a difficult time."
"I guess so."
It looks the same.
The Toe River lazily creeps along.
Alexis grabs my hand. Alexis swings my hand back and
forth. We stand under the old oak tree. Its limbs
are stiff and spiked.
The feed store is locked down. A sign says
knock or ring the bell if you want to buy something.
I do not knock. I just shake my head.

"Who'd buy feed out here?" "I don't know. There's
always been lots of horses. Dogs. Chickens. That
sort of thing. Farmland." "Doesn't look like it does
much business." "Nope." We stare at the windows.
They are covered in dust. The feed store is white.
The feed store is two stories with a basement cellar.
"Do you want to knock?" "No point." "You sure? This was
once the pharmacy or drugstore, right?" "Yep."
"You think?" "Not after all this time. No clues.
Maybe if I was a forensic scientist, but they had all that
stuff up here and they didn't find anything." "I still think
it had to do with the woman in the truck. The break in.
I think it had something to do with that. Plumtree doesn't
have a library does it?" I laugh. I shake my head. I kick my
shoes in the gravel. "All you see is here, is here. There's
nothing here. The mine employed people. The town
built up around it. When the mine closed down,
the town did, too. Who'd live here anyway unless they
were from here? Maybe a vacation home if you like
country living and isolation." Alexis sighs.
It feels the same.
The Toe River lazily creeps along.
"I'm knocking."
"Alexis, c'mon. Don't."
She knocks. She rings the bell. I look around the
valley. Not much had changed. The forests were thick
with green. The valley soaked with fog and clouds.
We stand. We wait for fifteen minutes. I circle the parking
lot four times. I walk over to the mine. It smells
like turpentine. I stare at the smokestacks. They
were peppered with holes and rusted out in most places.
Six minutes later, the door opens. A man with
a cigar, white hair, and glasses peers out.   He wears

a blue bathrobe.

"Did you knock?"

Alexis nods. "Yeah. We did."

"Don't stand out there all day. Come on in."
He shuffles backwards. He pulls open the door revealing
a large room filled with shelves of oats, barley, corn,
dog food, cat food, rabbit food, all kinds of animal food.
Alexis offers her hand. "I'm Alexis. This is Mikeal,
Uh, Mike." I hold out my hand. The old man stares at
me. Chews on his cigar. The old man tightens his
bathrobe and scratches his nose.

"Mikeal?" He scrunches his nose and squints his eyes.
"You're Mikeal Jacobson?"

I nod. Lean against the counter.

"Haven't seen you in these parts in a while."

"Yes, sir. Sorry, I don't know who—."

"You wouldn't. I knew your grand pappy.
He was a good man. Shame of what happened. It
was just terrible." "Yes. Yes, it was." "And they
never found out who did it, did they?" Alexis pipes
up from the corner. The old man shakes his head.

"Nope." He shuffles behind the counter. "I'm guessing
you two don't need no feed, is that about right?"
I nod and sigh. "I'm sorry, mister?" "Mister Edwards.
Just call me Old Ed. Everybody does."

"Okay. Old Ed. I'm sorry we bothered you. I just came
up here to do some—." "Research." Alexis pipes up
again. "Research?" He laughs. Old Ed scratches his chin.
The store creaks with the wind. "Trying
to resolve your grand pappy's ghost is that it? Folks
was wondering how long it'd take ya." I kick at the
floor. A mountain of dust rises around my feet.

"I'm not sure I'd call it that, but that's sort of it."

"Can you tell us anything about the woman who
was found in the back of the truck up at your town
square? Did she have anything to do with Ted's
estranged brother Mikeal's Great Uncle?"
Old Ed scratches his crotch.
"Ted's brother? I remember him. Eli. I think
that was the name?" I nod. "Yep. Eli." "Let's see,
I think Eli was married four or five times. Let's see,
It must've been four. No one ever claimed her, but
the rumor was that woman found in the truck, dead
you see, was wife number four. Eli brought her here
to Ted's farm to dispose of her. Used the far field
barn, you remember that one Mikeal? I don't think
it had been used in years. It was falling down. But
there was some meat hooks out there. Used them
to hang up meat to drain the blood. That body they
found had the life drained out of it."
"The woman in the truck?" Alexis's face turns white.
"Yep. But nobody cared about that."
"Whatever happened to Eli?" I stare at Old Ed.
"You don't know? I guess you wouldn't. Your
grand pappy wouldn't wanted you near the likes of him.
Rumor was that your grand pappy found him
in the far field barn, found out what he'd done and
run him out of town. Course he didn't leave. The next
day they found some of his clothes a floating up in the
Toe River. No one ever asked Ted or Rachel
if they knew anything. Everybody just figured
it was garbage one way or the other and that was that."
"And that was that?" Alexis echoes.
"And that was that."
It isn't the same.
The Toe River hastily rips along.

Chapter 19: The House

Cereal boxes.
Cardboard bible.
Windows are the eyes of the house.
Sagacious tower.
Home.
Residence.
Dwelling.
Abode.
Domicile.
Address.
Quarters.
Habitat.
Locale.
Environment.
Surroundings.
Territory.
Habitation.
Haunt.
Station.
Digs.
Lodgings.
Place of birth.
Place of origin.
Home town.
Birthplace.
Origin.
Source.
Native soil.
Home based.

Household.
Home-grown.
Family.
Domestic.
Homespun.
Home-made.
Home-produced.
Household.
Family.
Family circle.
Family unit.
Institution.
Relations.
Relatives.
People.
Folks.
Kin.
Children.
Ancestors.
Descendants.
Dynasty.
Lineage.
Line.
Family tree.

Chapter 20: The House, Part Two

The house is cold and damp

its smell overwhelming

I hear the squeak of mice, I think.

Alexis shines a flashlight in my face.

"There's no electricity?"

I shrug my shoulders. "What would be the point? I never come

here."

"It's been how long? Five years? You could

put it on the market and move it now. Sell it to the place that

says

they'd make it into a health spa. Fresh coat of paint. Remodel

something.

You could say newly remodeled. That always works."

"Price reduced?" "That'd probably work, too."

Alexis grins

Alexis pushes me forward.

I stumble into the kitchen. She shines the flashlight.

"Which room were they?"

"I don't know if I remember. But, they weren't together."

"Two different rooms? They were surprised?"

"Rachel was in the living room. Sewing. Ted.

Let's see. He may have been in the bedroom. I don't remem-

ber. It's

probably in your file." "I left it in the car." "Right." "It doesn't

really

matter, does it? Where they found them? The bodies were

probably moved." "What makes you say that?"

I pull a dust cover off a sofa

a cloud of dust billows up in my face.

I cough. Alexis waves her hands in front of her face.
"You should just leave all this stuff covered
but you should have it all removed.
It's not salvageable." "Yeah, but look." Alexis shines the
flashlight
on the sofa. Dark stains were splattered in a haphazard fashion.
"Blood stains. Still here. That wouldn't be a selling point."
"I just didn't know what to do with it all."
Alexis grabs my arm. We use the low light from her flashlight
to search the house room by room.
A flicker of sunshine filters in through the windows. Back down
in
the living room, Alexis grabs my hand and squeezes it. "You
think
I'm too old for you, don't you?" I shake my head.
"What are you talking about?" Alexis sighs. "It's not just about
my
file. The TV movie or screenplay, this trip. I mean is it? I
thought
maybe you liked me a little." I scratch my head. "I do
like you Alexis. But you could have anybody, why would you be
interested in—."
Alexis grabs my face
Alexis kisses me.
A long wet slow kiss like I know she practiced on her leading
men in her
movies. A long hot warm kiss like I had seen her do in the
movies.
A long sweet kiss that ends too soon. "Mike. Mikeal. Gosh, I'm
sorry. I don't know what came over me. It's all this history.
The
house is a wonderful house if not for its history. An old farm-
house.

Just like out of a fairytale." "It's okay. I—."

"C'mon, let's get out of here. There aren't any answers here anymore. It's been too long, right?"

Alexis grabs my hand

Alexis pulls me towards the door.

I jerk her hand back. She shuffles her feet.

"Mike. What the—!" "Shh. Alexis, wait a minute. Hold on. Let me have your

flashlight." She hands it to me careful

to avoid our fingers touching.

I grab it and shine it in the kitchen. I search three of the four drawers

before I find it. I hold it up in the light. "What is it?" I look down at the thick white notebook. "It's nothing. It's

Rachel's address book. Maybe there's something in there worth a look.

Maybe something to do with this Eli Old Ed told us about."

"C'mon. It's getting late. I'm starving."

"Yeah, me too."

I hold the book out to Alexis.

Alexis takes the address book and clutches it to her chest.

Chapter 21: Rachel's Address Book

Rachel's book is simply that. Scrawled names in her perfectly
illegible handwriting.
Names. Dates. Phone numbers. All in pencil. Smudged. The
sheets
yellowed. After all this time. Old Ed hands us a phone book and
shakes his head.
"The police went through that thing you know. You didn't
find anything no one else did. Why don't you just let it rest,
Mikeal?
Give the folks of Plumtree a break."
I glare at him
I stare at him.
"Are you telling me something Old Ed?
Was the town responsible for what happened to my grandpar-
ents?
Did they cover it up?
Alexis looks up at this
Alexis studies Old Ed
Alexis flips through her folder.
She had nothing on him. Her file amounted to
what anyone could find on the internet
or a newspaper microfiche.
Old Ed hands us a cup of coffee. I sip mine. Alexis sits down
on
the floor. "It's gettin' late you know. If you're gonna make the
drive
back to Beech Mountain you'd better get started less you wanna
try it
in the dark." I glare at Old Ed. "I grew up here.

I know how to get back to Beech Mountain. Sure the road's
curvy
and dips down by the stream, but I've been on it lots of times.
It's a simple drive."
"Yeah, but even so when it's late
or if you're tired
it's easy to
make mistakes."
Old Ed glares at me
old Ed stares at me.
"Are you saying what I think you're saying that somebody made
a mistake. That's all it was. A simple mistake?"
Old Ed pulls up a stool. Nods to Alexis.
"Why'nt you put that folder away. There
ain't nothing in there that's gonna help you. The police just did a
formal investigation cause of who your grandparents were. They
couldn't ignore it. Don't you remember I told you about Eli?
How he disappeared? He was hiding out at that cabin right
by the house barn on the way to the far field barn.
Your grand pappy had let him stay. But Rachel.
She was a simple good woman.
She found out about it.
Anyway, the story goes that Eli just disappeared."
"I believe you said his clothes
were found floating in the Toe River." "Yep, that's it." "But
that's not
what really happened to him, is it?" I drain my coffee in one
swift gulp. "You want more coffee?" Old Ed holds up the pot.
I shake my head. "I've had enough." "It's simple really.
I guess we all thought it'd be better if you didn't know. If no one
knew. You especially, Mikeal, after what happened to your
mother."
"I can see that," Alexis mumbles. "Why wouldn't the

police do something?" "Well, they might've but no one knew what happened to Eli. That is the truth. It was his clothes they found floating. Only it was after—. Well, it was after what happened to Rachel and Ted." "Ted and Rachel?" I scratch my head. "Rachel wanted Eli gone?

They suspected he killed his wife right here on the old homestead.

But Ted, he let Eli stay. Is it that simple?"

"Hid him in the cabin from the law's more like it.

Ted always said that no matter what Eli was his brother.

Case closed. As simple as that."

"And Eli's family?"

"They really didn't come looking for him if there was a family.

Probably not. He didn't stick with a woman long enough to father

any children." "It's as simple as that?"

I scratch my nose

I squeeze my coffee cup.

"It's as simple as that."

Old Ed nods his head and shrugs his shoulders.

"It's as simple as that.

Alexis slams her folder shut and sighs.

"Case closed." "No movie?"

"It's enough to work with."

"No one knows what happened to Eli?"

Old Ed sighs. "They know. No one's talking."

"As simple as that?"

"As simple as that."

Chapter 22: Nothing's As Simple As It Seems

"Do you believe him?" Alexis locks the door to the Wagoneer.
She nods and waves to Old Ed. "Do you?" "Don't see that we have

a choice." I nod and wave to Old Ed. "He made it clear."
"You think he killed them?" "Doesn't seem likely looking
at him now, but who knows."
I flip on the radio.
Alexis flips it off.
"Mikeal. Come on." I start the engine and stare at the
Toe. It gurgles in my rearview mirror. It is wide and brown
and at one time there had been large stones in the water. There was

a wet path or shortcut from the general store to the cabin that sat on

my grandparents homestead. I look for the stones. I do not see them.
I shut off the engine. I jump out of the car. "Mikeal! Where are
you—?"
Old Ed shakes his head and laughs. He thinks I'm going to pee
behind the bushes.
I run past the feed store
I run past the house
I run to the cabin where Ted had hidden Eli.
The roof has fallen.
The porch sags.
I run to the path.
I stare at the water.
I look for the stones. The wide round stones.

The river is wider.
The river is rougher.
The river is wilder.
I drop to my knees. I look for the stones.
Old Ed comes up behind me. Alexis follows. She is breathing
loudly.
"You won't find what you're looking for in the river."
I lean back. I stare at the old man.
"The stones? What happened to the stones? Remember?"
Old Ed shakes his head. "You did grow up here, more or less
didn't
you? It took you all these years to notice." "They're gone?
They
were removed?" Old Ed nods. Old Ed points towards the
general store.
"Wasn't like they were gettin' much use after the store closed
anyway.
Specially when what's my feed store today was made into a
general
store. Didn't need two of 'em." "It was all about a general
store?
Sales? Profit?" "Like I said, Mikeal. Didn't need two stores. A
place
the size of Plumtree's lucky to support one much less two."
"This was
all about cheese, bread, milk, meat, shoes, clothing, stuff like
that?"
"And feed. Don't forget feed." "But your feed store, it was a
pharmacy
at the time of the murders, right?" Alexis drops to her knees.
Alexis looks
into the gurgling brown river water. "Folks have a long memory
up in

the hills. You Hollywood types, what would you know about that?”

I look at Alexis. “He means it’s a feud like thing. Something that went on some time back.” “Yep. Sort of. Your grand pappy sold

his land for the second general store that became a pharmacy.” “That became the feed store?” “That became your feed store?” I ask the second question. I stand up and hold out my hands to Alexis. She jumps to her feet. “What did it matter to you? To your family?” “Didn’t matter that much, but it was my chance

for a start. A fresh start.” Alexis’ eyes go wide. I see the whites

of her eyes. “That was your wife found dead in front of the old general store. Why your—.” “Yep. That’s right. I’m Eli.” “Eli!”

I stare at him. I stare real good. I see no family resemblance. I see none at all. “You—.” “Mikeal. Give it a rest. I’m giving you

this one last chance.” “Your clothes were found floating in the Toe.” Alexis’ eyes are wider. “How is this possible?”

“You’re right. It was my clothes. Eli’s clothes. They don’t belong to me now. I made a fresh start. Turned over a new

leaf. I’ve committed colloquialism after colloquialism.”

Alexis stares

Alexis’ feet are planted in the grass.

I nod to Old Ed

I nod to Eli.

I hold out my hands to Alexis.

“Alexis, come on. Let’s be on our way.”

“But—.”

“Alexis! Come on. Let’s be on our way.”

Old Ed's face stares into my rearview mirror.
Eli's snarl spits on my bumper.
Alexis grips the folder
Alexis opens the window and tosses it out.
"Let them find that floating in the Toe."
"Yeah" is the only word I can muster.
"Yeah" is the only thing I say on the drive back to
Beech Mountain.
"Yeah" is the only thing I think about while we
pack our bags and sleep with the lights
on in our rented rooms.

Chapter 23: Elimination

It's quiet. It's very quiet. There is no
noise in the Wagoneer. Little to no noise
in the Wagoneer. Alexis sleeps. I drive.
She sleeps and I drive some more. I drop
her off at the house in Columbia. She
says to me there will not be a movie, no
one would believe any of it anyhow. I
want to tell her she sounds southern. I tell
her I understand and that maybe other ideas
will come along. Old Ed tells me I need to
sell the old homestead. He sends me pictures
of the house being bulldozed, but not in
such a way that the whole house is gone.
The frame is removed. The inside
of the house still standing. He writes that
the new outside will be brick. Alexis finishes
her play and moves out, back to Hollywood.
She takes the cat, the one blue eyed cat with her.
She leaves no forwarding address. I know
she thinks I'm friends with a murderer. I
know she thinks that I'm kin to Old Ed aka
Eli so that I'm related to a murderer. I always
liked Alexis. Nothing against her. What she
doesn't know, what she never learns won't hurt
her. It won't hurt her. It will never hurt her.
Old Ed is not Old Ed.
Old Ed is not Eli either.
Old Ed does not exist.
Eli really did disappear.

Old Ed is an actor named Mack
something or other.
Rachel's address book is simply a
prop, a notebook that can be bought at
a drugstore, gas station and filled up with
made up names scribbled in pencil.
Old Ed is a a retired actor
I hired to retire in Plumtree
to own and run the feed store
and forget his real name.
Old Ed thinks I hired him
to boost the property
value, to erase the memories of the murders
to impersonate Eli if anyone ever pried too deeply.
He's partially right. I did hire him to erase.
But I hired him to erase for me, to wipe
it all out, to wipe out what I did to my own
grandparents so I could inherit young
so I could kite surf or whatever so I could
answer the question if I was really like my
no good Daddy like they were always telling
me and so I could do things like hang out
with Alexis and her one blue eyed cat and
so I could be left to clean up the past, and
left to my beach in Hatteras where I watch the
kite surfers all day every day seven days a week,
waiting for another renter to find the house
in Columbia and see how far we get along
and see how well we get along and see just
how far we get along with or without Rachel and Ted.

-The End

About the Author

L.B. Sedlacek

LB Sedlacek has had poetry, fiction and non-fiction appear in many different journals, zines and newspapers. She is a former Poetry Editor for "ESC! Magazine" and also co-hosted the podcast for the small press, "Coffee House to Go." She teaches poetry workshops at local elementary and middle schools. Recent poetry books include "Happy Little Clouds" (Guerrilla Genesis Press)" and "The Poet Next Door" (Cyberwit). Her first short story collection came out on Leap Day 2020 entitled "Four Thieves of Vinegar & Other Short Stories" published by Alien Buddha Press.   In her free time, LB enjoys swimming, reading, and playing guitar and ukulele.

ALSO BY LB SEDLACEK

POETRY
Alexandra's Wreck *Kitty Litter Press*
Constellate *GoatsonMars Press*
Happy Little Clouds *Guerrilla Genesis Press*
Hey Astro! GoatsonMars Press
Mars or Bust *GoatsOnMars Press*
Poetry in LA – Only in LA *GoatsonMars Press*
The Adventures of Stick People on Cars *Alien Buddha Press*
The Architect of French Fries *Presa Press*
The Poet Next Door *Cyberwit*
Words and Bones *Finishing Line Press*

FICTION
The Glass River
The Mailbox of the Kindred Spirit
Traveling with Fish

NON-FICTION
Bridge Ices Before Road
Electric Melt
The Catnip Gene
The Traveling Postcard

FOR MORE INFORMATION
L.B. Sedlacek
http://www.lbsedlacek.com
Facebook: @lbsedlacekpoet
Twitter: @lbsedlacek
Instagram: @lbsedlacek

9 789388 319300